November Adrenaline

Published by Goldfish Press
4545 42nd Avenue Southwest
Suite 211
Seattle, Washington, 98116

Manufactured in the United States of America

ISBN-13: 978-0971259805
ISBN-10: 0971259801

Library of Congress Card Number: 2018930825

Cover & Book Design by Koon Woon

This book was set on the Monotype Book Antiqua

November Adrenaline

Poems by John W. Gorski

Goldfish Press
Seattle

Table Of Contents

Part I. *A Million Suns in His Head*

Part II. *Beachless*

Part III. *Unfinished Collage 1972*

Part IV. *A City of Pre-Raphaelite Strangers*

Part I

A Million Suns in His Head

Agoraphobia

The Baltimore sky hung
automobile exhaust
above Gwynn Oak amusement park
that summer evening.
People approached at angles
in streaming intersections,
as I heard the roar
of the roller coaster
carrying laughter and screams.

Then I saw a boy my age
pass by wearing a dark red
Tyrolean hat with a white feather
making the first crack
that in later years would be filled
by crowded rooms electric
with sinister gazes.

Why that ostentation
agitated me I can't say
as I look back
at that fog of Ferris wheels.

Identity Loss at the Movies

Down a summer street off Myrtle Avenue
in Brooklyn near the El station,
I watch an Oriental epic
in the charcoal hush of the Ritz Theater
while thinking of the first feature about Joan of Arc.
Somewhere in the celluloid haze,
I've dropped my paper school ID card.
Outside, I fidget through my pockets –
crows circling in my thoughts,
hectoring in Anglicized German:
"How could you be so careless;
why didn't you use your head?"

Years later, it will be found
in a layer of soot – a smiling fifteen-year-old
in a button-down head shot revealed
by then as a mask burned away
at the stake of daily life.

On the screen, Chinese porters carry
supplies over the border of a mountain pass
of craggy rock and abyss sky
aflame with the Tibetan sun
whose billion facets I would enter
through colored tablets I swallowed
in my early twenties.
The ignited kindling at my feet
would rise into my brain
with more knowledge than I could program
and I'd start to wonder if my mirror image was real.

But at eighteen, I'd already begun
to fall out of lockstep
with the other soldiers and sense
their jeers before they spoke –
trains coming from blocks away,
shaking the upper windows of the neighborhood.

Polaroid Journey Back

I'm going back to
the Polaroid length
of the Delaware river.
Standing by its overcast shore
in Wilmington with my grandmother
who mutters in German,
I am four years old
and less than three feet tall –
an unwitting replica
of Trudy Montag's main squeeze.

Tonight, I'm looking through
black and white photographs
of my first ten years,
watching my lack of stature
and downcast face winding back
to its headwaters.

The camera's droll eye
catches me bow-tied
in white shirt and Sunday school slacks
a few years later –
a living room quarterback
ready to throw a football
while looking towards the floor:
"Hey, go out for a long one,
if you really want to,"
it seems to say.

Or there I am at the front door
of our Maryland address
in the uniform of a space man
pointing a ray gun
at the other dime store-costumed invaders
from down the block.

And though I eventually reached
the height of 5′ 6″,
there was a swift current
that ran through me
carrying the same sentiment
of the protagonist in "The Tin Drum"
who never wanted to grow up.

Ancestral Reverb

The rivers of Middle Tennessee
have devious currents that can
drag a body to rest.
So, he never wanted his eight children
to learn how to swim.

"Wood does not cost nothing,"
he exclaimed to the sawdust circus
of his sons running around
his shop, knocking over
a cane backed chair he was working on.
In the Great Depression, he was trying to feed
his family on a cabinet maker's wages.

He loved the stained glass sun
streaming on Sunday mornings
but not the starched white certainties
of his mother's church that counted
only sinners outside its sect.
He read Poe stories and painted
as a young man until one day
he took a razor to his canvasses.
It was the night river thoughts drowning him,
the 2 a.m. freight train out of Nashville
with its unbearable, blaring horn
that came with his heritage.

He knew about the translucent hill people,
miles to the east who plucked
out "Barbra Allen" on banjo
and guitar in the pitch black hours

the same way it had been brought over
from Scotland centuries before –
a music that sounded in his insomnia.

Decades later, when his eldest daughter
witnessed the dawn horizon
as a seam of coal,
she heard his voice telling her to look west.

John W. Gorski

Witness of Stones

The shouts and cries stirred vault tones
in the granite of our megaliths
that hooded night on the greensward above the sea.

There was a man caught in a circle of knives
stabbing into his robe – a garden of roses
in the atonality of a dark opera.
We sensed it was the village scribe
who had vexed the hearts of some with his satire
and so they crucified his wit and tossed
the body into the black Atlantic
crashing at this margin of Britain.

Later, we heard he sailed
over the waves to a distant century
in middle America where he looked
out through the blue eyes
of a newborn that grew to
a young man who went insane
with a million suns in his head.

James Dean's Sister

Seen through a fisheye
lens in a Greenwich Village walk up,
James Dean lounges in a chair –
floating in the smoky haze
of a Charlie Parker sax solo –
reeling back to the bronze-gold bridges
over an azure Seine
and the Parisian cellar club
where he played bongos in a satin shirt,
a cigarette clenched in his teeth.

He went out to Hollywood.
She stayed in Indiana
amid the warehouses and rail yards
under low riding clouds that blew in
on a cold wind from the Plains.

Many summers, I would see her
walking down Main Street,
wilting in flowered dresses.
She was only famous around here
and in conversations with herself.
When I grew older, I hung out
with her in all night diners.
Caught in the glow
of her Babel Juke Box
powered by voltage of hearsay,
I looked into
her neon derisive eyes.

Weary of that town,
I dreamed far to the west
where serotonin gulls lifted
above cedar-fringed harbors.

Pictures from an Infernal Season

In Rotterdam, you climb a blackening ladder
up to a cave where the alcohol trance beats
of White Zombie pound the walls and floor
of a room dim in amber light.
There young tuxedos and buxom girls
in low cut dresses lounge around cerise
tables, drinking and smoking.
Everyone is getting wasted – stranded
in faux satanic wisecracks and jibes
at their parents whom they dread becoming.

Then they rise in white clothes to a field
of Dutch mud that stains their legs and ankles,
as they tramp and dance around.
Suddenly, they hug – realizing
their formal education is over.

Daydreaming in an Illuminated World

Dead yellow grasses poke through the mantle
of snow everywhere in the Netherlands
this day under wilted, cauliflower light.

The Turkish resident worker has the day off.
He sits in a rundown Amsterdam hotel,
his back to a white table cloth
stained by wine – a purple drool
that spilled in his sleeping head last night.
A window brings in overcast etched in frost.
In a corner, a couch beckons with the pink,
plush contours of the inside of an oyster.

There, he can nod off and dream
of a Black Sea resort far from
these wintry streets arguing in a Germanic tongue.

Cezanne – Refused

Year after year, his entries turned down
by the Salon, he yearned for Provence.
While strolling under the chimney smoke
and sallow sunlight of Paris, he pictured
to himself the violet-gray clouds
wreathing Mt. St. Victorie
and the red roofs spilling to the Mediterranean.

For days, he labored in his atelier
on a single still life -
the green of pears cooling his fierce mind,
the scarlet apples igniting his heart.
He said, "Art should tell us what the eye thinks."

In his final years,
after an auction of his work in Aix,
copies of the local newspaper's critical review
were left at his doorstep by
some of the town's middle class.
Attached to them were messages
asking him to leave the village
"he was dishonoring" with the lurid colors
and slanting angles of his canvasses.

So, he tramped north over
the bleached out meadows of the valley –
the bourgeois howls still blackening his thoughts –
to his cabin on the side
of the limestone mountain.
Withdrawn in the swarthy shadows
of his studio there, he continued

the raw-hued tilt of his subjects –
his gaze and brush siring the visions
of Matisse and Picasso.

Leopardi di Giacoma

He grew up in the palazzo
of his father
under the cold,
scheming eyes of his mother –
chained to her piety
and the sainthood she saw in him.
A sickly child,
he escaped into the tomes
of his father's library
and read the classics
whose heroes soared
in his mind's eye
on the wings of eagles,
as he became a prodigy
of languages.

Out on the cobble-stoned street,
he heard the silver peal
of the neighbor girl
singing at her loom –
a music like daylight
that seemed to go on forever.
But in a few years,
winter branches grew
in her tubercular lungs,
until she could not breathe.

He felt alone again
on warm summer afternoons –
imprisoned by a hedge that blocked
the shining Adriatic
so he could only imagine it.

Then he returned
to his shadowy room,
a candelabra of poems
lit in his head
that guided his pen.

The ideals of the young scholar
sank on disintegrating wings
when he first encountered Rome
where the cathedral of St. Peter
shone above carousels
of tenements and filthy alleys.

He could sense nothing
beyond the final beat of his heart
while he declined in many rooms –
listening to the long-
skirted laughter of women
on the sidewalks outside.

His waxen face
and bedridden body
float toward us now
from his last photograph.

Message from Crysta

Crysta keeps on
talking, although her hair
is on fire.
She smokes one cigarette
after another
to calm the voices
that tell her to die.

Today, she is staying in,
drinking red wine
to avoid falling into
the cellar filled with hyena cries
waiting in the spaces
between sidewalk conversations.

She is writing a poem
in a scratchy
indecipherable language,
as if she were still alive.

Waking in the shrouded
light of morning,
this is the message
I get from her.

She wants to be heard.

Three Sketches

Mark

I always wondered what happened to him.
We went to the junior high sock hops on Friday nights
with two girls from our neighborhood in Severna Park;
we sampled Banana cordial and Kentucky bourbon
at neighbors' houses when Mark babysat their children.
One of them had a son – an apprentice Eddie Haskell
who saw us hitchhiking on the highway to Annapolis
and told our parents. I was grounded for a week.
Mark got two weeks. So he had to practice piano every
day after school. The next year, 1963, he learned 'Foggy
Mountain Breakdown' on the banjo. I sat there in my
envy and fake Madras shirt while he played hay trucks
rattling down winding roads and silver-throated rapids
descending shrouded heights of the Blue Ridge. In 1964,
he witnessed the major/minor chord epiphany of the
Beatles. He grew his hair long and formed a band called
"The Sheep." Then my family moved to Cincinnati and
we lost touch. In 1967, I heard he dropped out of the
University of Maryland and was drafted and sent to
Vietnam.

Gerard

He wandered in from Avondale – Cincinnati's ghetto –
and hung out around Bill's head shop that summer
of 1969. He was 40 and wore an African robe.
I recall his angry, mahogany face under
a broad-brimmed black hat when some of the hippie
kids there laughed at his fey mannerisms.
Sometimes, they took his ornamental walking staff
and he threatened to put a curse on them,
claiming to be a warlock.
He was an artist and liked to stow his paintings
behind the counter at Bill's head shop. One night,
I looked at two of them. The first was a still life
of a beige nude in a double aura sitting sideways by
a rainy blue window. The other showed a lunar
landscape with a pool of blood ringed by silver
crampons. That autumn, I saw him in a dream
stretching his arms until they encompassed a lake
in a forest. Three or four years later,
one of my brother's friends said
he saw Gerard, in another part of town,
wearing Super Fly fashions. Then he heard Gerard
went home one day and swallowed
a bottle of shaving lotion and died.

Sheila

The glow of her cigarette was the only light left as the
summer day burned out over the apartment buildings
of her neighborhood near the University of Cincinnati.
She was schizophrenic and 41, 13 years older than me.
Her hair had gone gray from a long reign of
psychodrama. I had met her in 1975 in an outpatient
program. The next year, I lived three blocks away from
her for a few months before I left for Seattle.
We hung out sometimes and talked about poetry.
She liked to read the Confessional poets.
Every once and awhile, she managed to write – a few
lines creeping from the locked-down ward of her mind
on anti-psychotic meds, drifting out like Ohio river fog -
filtering a ray of Sexton heartache.

Too Much Information – Route #174

Rolling past the sidewalk crowds
pulsing like graffiti
in the gray air, she says,
"These people scare me
with their cheeks rouged in gun powder
and white skulls painted
on the shoulders of their black leather coats
and wine-red eyes
that burn right through you.

Then this morning,
there was this lady
with a little dark circle
on her forehead
like those people from India;
it reminded me of that black sun
back home in Alabama
that used to hide
behind a copper face in the evening.

I'll feel better when I get home
and take my medicine."

Then the bus driver turned
halfway around and said,
"Too much information."

Metro Prophet – 3rd Ave., Seattle

"The storm will kill two
out of three people on earth
with three hundred mile-per-hour winds –
celestial winds
and tremors in the ground
that open in gulfs of fire," he said.

In a "Road Warrior" coonskin cap
and mutton chops,
he preached from a seat
in the "tilt-a-whirl" center
of the articulated bus.

"The warnings of this sage
have come true in the past,"
he said, as we rode through
the daguerreotype gray
of the city streets.

After a while, he noticed
my slumped shoulders
and dog food eyes
and as I got up to leave,
he said, "Be happy."

Monster, Chiller, Horror Theater

I went to bed early that April
evening and hid my head
under the covers – afraid
of the neon hologram devil
hovering with a glowing spear
pointed at me.

The next afternoon, I fell down a well
into a movie theater
in Glen Burnie where I impaired
my future dental health
on the hard caramel of Sugar Daddies
while I watched sailors gambling for dynamite sticks
to throw at the shelled invaders
in "The Attack of the Giant Crab Monsters."

The second feature was about
a plastic surgeon at a private hospital
who operated on beautiful models –
transforming them to gargoyles.
When he took off his dark glasses,
his patients screamed upon
witnessing the white lagoons of his eyes
missing their pupils.

Thinking of those unearthly orbs,
I ran home along
the old Baltimore and Annapolis Road –
leery of the night enveloping the brick
and white fronts of the suburban homes.

The next morning, I stepped
into the light – a moon-bitten child
with my brother on the way
to Sunday school in matching gray,
blue, and cream plaid "aren't we dorky" suits.

Petit Memoirs, 1964-1970

Masks

I recall the eyes of our family cat:
green fluorescent dimes looking through
the mask of basement stairs dark in 1968.
She was luckier than her predecessors,
watching color TV with us while they
peered at the masked man and Tonto
riding across the screen of our old black and white
RCA. She chose us well at the S.P.C.A.,
knowing that my parents both had good jobs –
so she would never wind up on food stamps.

Lace Curtains

Their veils blew in
through the bedroom windows facing Lytle Street –
carried by the cool 10 a. m.
Tennessee breeze that August, 1964.
I was staying with my grandmother
after my grandfather had died in April;
she said she still saw him in the hall
at unexpected moments.
Until the last year, he'd worked in his shop
restoring antique furniture for the moneyed
women of Murfreesboro whom he referred
to as the "cornbread aristocracy" and sometimes
"old heifers"when my grandmother relayed
the harangue of their phone calls.
He chewed tobacco and worked amid wood dust
and lacquer fumes that entered his lungs,
and then his brain, until an Alzheimer's fugue
began to play and he sang along with
Beatles' tunes on the radio –
"She loves you, yeah, yeah, yeah."

Ritual Ground (England)

Ghosted by Druids, the pond inscribes
the centuries-old copse of trees around it
like countless pictures from the collective
unconscious that emerged
on magazine and album covers in the late 60's.
Words like "sea" and "sky" and "soul" used to stand
out in bold type and then buzz quietly in books I read
after I had dropped acid a few times
and smoked hash for a year or so.
There was a dark woods in the linoleum block print
my brother made for an art class in 1970;
in a clearing, there was a tree stump of knotted muscle
tattooed with the face of a blackened clock –
a sight E. A. Poe might have encountered
in one of his stories.

Pictures from Lost Sleep

1. Monochrome Monday Memory

The two clerical workers fret in their cubicles under the milky-gray purgatory of office lights. Their passwords aren't allowing them to access their program in Rom-Dos on this morning in 1987. So they're resigned to this scenario from a C. S. Lewis novel of the future that could, at least, imagine this particular color of tedium.

2. Lynwood Time Warp

The maiden with the silver wind chime earrings likes her music without syncopation in the cool patchouli forest of evening. It is where she looks to for sanctuary, after casting off the deathly trance orchestra vibrating her boyfriend's headphones. There she reads the I Ching by the flame of a Bic lighter and unwraps the tiny scroll of the lavender-scented horoscope she picked up at Seven-Eleven. She seeks out the stars for the reasons why men are so weird.

3. Skating to the End of Days

He advances with his feet in empty boxes of dry Hispanic noodles mounted on roller skate wheels. Shoe leather has become scarce with Armageddon near. He speeds up through the adobe neighborhoods half-eaten by centuries of storms in the past two weeks. Under heavens humming with a million vacuum cleaners, he rolls on in tandem with the final dog, a moth-eaten old hound, who yelps the riffs to "All Along the Watchtower."

Fear of Heights

One day in second grade, I watched
children on the swing sets
vaulting into the blue
above the sandy, Maryland ground;
a classmate standing by said
"If you go over the top of the set,
you'll break your neck."
My mother warned me never to go out
in a thunderstorm because lightning bolts
would come down like a swing seat
and pitch me into heaven.

In Aden, Rimbaud walked
past a grimy, half open door
splattered with black serpent script
where Abyssinians passed a pipe
of smoldering hashish.
Then he recalled a night in Paris
years before when he stared
with stoned eyes into a mirror
at his disembodied gaze.

In the next century, I looked from
my bedroom window at the back yard
of faded Ohio winter grass –
growing dark with the teeming dead.
The walls were tapestried
with ancient Tibetan faces – galleries of deep,
fixed eyes radiating on and off.
I was freaking out on a half tab
of acid cut with speed, waiting for
my mother to get home from work.

When she arrived, I told her to call
the hospital because I was going to die.
Instead, she gave me a couple Sominex
and I found some old Thorazine
and soon slipped into blotto land.

The following day, I still heard canyons
opening in the chord changes
of a Jefferson Airplane track.
But the high waned
as the hours fell into night.

Paging Llewyn Davis

He is a striding 6'1'' with anthracite
locks fringing his collar, an eternal 24-year-old
with a rust-flecked razor growl
delineating the blues in Greenwich Village,
outshining the bard of the Mesabi range.

He serenades the Botticelli angels
of MacDougal Street in 1961.
Fifty years later, I catch myself
humming sea chanties in the mirror
until green linoleum voices groan
and a teenage neighbor turns on Grand Auto Theft.
He teaches guitar while I only strum
chords and can't keep time in 1964 –
a schlemiel playing schlemieleonic changes
on a 6-string from Sears and Roebuck.

Llewyn sips from laudanum teacups
in 1963 and never gets hauled in
by Manhattan's boys in blue.
Me and my brother's musician friends
get busted with inferior Mexican weed
and weak opiated hash by the Dorfs
and Bachs and Schneiders of Cincinnati's finest.
I start going to bed early
and my court-appropriate, shorn hair
makes the needle skip
when I play "A Saucerful of Secrets"
on our Magnavox stereo;
he stays up all night
listening to the vinyl juke joint of Howlin' Wolf.

He haunts YouTube, as I age
behind aviator glasses –
a wannabe still buzzing in my head –
using Songify to turn my poems
into wails from a madhouse planet
no one would ever want to visit.

Blue Memory

I picture her smooth flesh
against mine
in the waking entrance
of the numberless overcast
of a late winter day.

The fragrance of her hair
and the positions
of her naked body
focus in my thought –
streaming echoes
of her love cries
and narrow face
turning in a kaleidoscope
of expression.

And then I grow tired
of the distance
of recollection and get up,
leaving this blue memory
to pass into nothingness.

Night River Music

In the early January nightfall,
the treble and bass
of cars and trucks flow like a river
past my window
while I listen to the million facets
of California sunlight that play
on my iPhone from a track
by the Quicksilver Messenger Service
circa 1968. The guitarist riffs
a tangle of expanding notes
on a Brubeck standard
that spin invisible vortices
amid a Golden Gate Park crowd.

Outside, the pavement curses
seem benign as I listen
to Steely Dan –
taking me down noir alleys
of shadowy people that thread
through LA neon.
Ocher mountains recede to the east
while shot glasses clink
in night clubs and the Pacific surf
is erased by trumpets and saxophones.

From an outdoor café
in the Hudson River valley,
Tim Hardin's wine-stained voice
pours into an April afternoon –
his breath filled with a lament
for a love that "will never happen again."

Muse Dictations – Dark and Light

I

"Hey, Mr. Halloween Paper Bag Masked
Man with knife slits for the broken
window panes you peer through,
we two dervishes would like a word," they said.

"Remember that county fair in Missouri
when the calliope's notes morphed
into cries of predator birds in the Ozarks
and the mornings of rattling Els
screeching to a halt at Wyckoff Avenue
where the passengers descended
to the Lethe of tunnels lit
by subways going to Manhattan.
Let's not forget the sky
above the Ohio River shrieking with
guitar feedback – the sound track
to the breaking glass of your consciousness,"
the first exclaimed.

"The hats we wear herald our gravestones
and you are one in billions,
an echo of dust to be lost
again in the whirlwind of our dance, "
the second one said.

II

"Do you want to talk?" the old woman
in the wheelchair said – a flickering gray-
green presence in the waking winter dawn.

"You came from me and I told
you about the cedar wind along
Lebanon Pike east of Nashville.
I gave you a book
that blazed with the Arles sun
and cooled with the mauve shadows of Giverny."

"I rode with you to the eternity
of Atlantic surf rolling in and out
off the coast of Maryland,
so you could one day hear
the Pacific calm to choir voices
at the mouth of the Columbia."

Part II

Beachless

Anne Arundel Kaleidoscope

Maltravers, Jump, Dale and Amberly -
funny names that giggled in my head,
carried across the sea centuries before,
now painted on the street signs
I passed by on the way home.
I strutted my fourth-grade self
through Harundale to the pre-fab
on a concrete slab in the post-war
planned community where we lived.

The cold, dark winter of "Heart Break Hotel"
had vacated and now
the chorus of "Youngblood" rang
from a convertible of teenagers
bound for the Baltimore-Annapolis Road
and the river inlets of the Chesapeake.
It was a late Saturday morning
in May as I ambled on,
jostling root-beer barrels
in my mouth and looking up
at the miracle
of a Pizarro-blue sky
streaked with cirrus clouds.

Neighborhood kids approached
down the sidewalk on roller skates and bikes –
an Armada of laughter and screams.
A Studebaker motored by –
trailing a line of carbon monoxide
and I thought of the perspiring rose
twilights of the summer to come

when we would line up
at the Good Humor truck
and munch on ice cream bars
tinged with exhaust fumes.

Sleep Waiting – Vignettes

The boatman in his summer uniform
appears each twilight in every season –
looking aside by a frothing Atlantic.
A dying pewter sun winks
above his shoulders as he waits
with folded arms for the servant class
who he is to carry into the stormy night
jostling their limbs with dreams.

The chimney sweep – grimy-faced and
soot-covered – stands in the marble hall
of a Manhattan manse
by a luxuriant house plant,
as an apprentice to consumption.

The handyman loiters
next to a mansion's walls,
glancing off into the boozed-up shadows –
an empty wine bottle
in the tool kit at his feet.

The white-aproned maid
holds the dust pan and brush
in the immaculate drawing room.
She stares through the window
at the silver motes dancing outside –
a scene her mistress in fancy hat
and brocade prepares to enter
on a pavement of human folly.

John W. Gorski

A white-haired man,
in a granite-gray suit,
walks through the Midtown crowds,
eager to merge with everyone
and everything he sees.
He wants to descend
with the strangers he observes
to the unconscious four a. m. depths
beyond the surf at Coney Island.

Loon Migration

If you listen you can hear
her playing a recorder
from a room where a Van Gogh hangs –
its Provence church rising alone
on a wheat-colored hill.
If you look you can see
her laughing in the family's backyard –
the August light lilting in her blond hair.

But you would have to see
past thousands of suns
to the loon's cry along the Chesapeake
that heralded Ohio skies
weighed with dulled bronze
and a voice stopped by marble.

The painting was lost
in storage years ago,
her record albums given away.
She was to have been married.

The wail has followed west
through decades on a tape loop
turning on again and again
with a plaint of cracked plaster
in an abandoned house
and the rime-hearted absence
for those that knew her.

The loon's baleful soundtrack
inhabits the brain of a man
who guides a pen in weather
rolling from the Pacific.

Beachless -- A Stone's Progress Out of Habitat

By the blue-green hiss of Cape Cod Bay
one morning, I came upon
a bleached, potato-shaped
stone–pitted and gray-speckled.
It lay on the beach surrounded
by kelp and the black skeletal length
of a dead horse shoe crab.

I brought it back in the family Chevrolet
to our prefab unit south of Baltimore,
to lie on a window sill alongside
a sea shell whispering an Atlantic hymn
that my mother acquired
from the sandy shore at Provincetown.

Later, it traveled with us
to subtropical summers
in the Ohio River Valley
where it sweated with every
thing animate and inanimate.
It wound up on an 85 degree
hardwood floor, nudged by athletic shoes,
while our collection of sea shells bided
their time on lacquered shelves,
haughty in the inner wash
of their ocean sounds.

It had become a door stop
in our Cincinnati home
but all our shoreline souvenirs
were trumped by the plastic shell
one of us bought in an East Barnstable gift shop
that played the wind-up music of the paean
Patti Page sang to the Cape.

Surveillance Eyes

Deploying a progeny of overseers,
its thousand visages were screens of electronic snow
that when gazed upon scrambled thoughts
and reveries into bar crowd noise;
its soulless vision neutralized
the dopamine of anyone in its thrall.

Looking into the gray fluorescence
of our morning room group therapy
at David, it followed him out
through rainy, purgatory streets
in First Hill where he wondered if
laughter he heard was aimed at him.
David would beg off the proffered joint
since his teenage years when he
and his friends smoked a lid a day.
At night, he would drive through South Seattle
with his girlfriend, listening to Bowie tapes,
trying to escape jeering winks of strangers.

Marlene from the group was twice divorced –
had epilepsy so bad she couldn't work.
She took the 150 home each day to her clapboard house
where she complained about neighbors
stealing from her and watched detective shows
on a balky TV with a plastic fork taped to its antenna.

Another outpatient, Joe, muttered
about people giving him the "Evil Eye"
and lolled in liquid window
afternoons of his Holly Park unit,
playing stacks of Zeppelin and AC-DC.

We waited for days that erased the fog -
when blue hills of dawn rose
with a sunburst of guitar chords
and we could hear the Elizabethan jazz altitudes
of "A Remark You Made."

Aint Angie

Earth convulsing with artillery rounds
and sky of droning aeroplanes
sounded in her fitful sleep.
She read about war across the Atlantic
every morning in the Nashville Banner
and saw black columns of vehicles
glaring Middle Tennessee daylight,
carrying home motionless soldiers
from the fields of France in 1918.

She lay under green sun-bright maples
in the town's park and listened to the distant
applause of their leaves, not sensing the storm to
come, decades away, when the hand claps would go
crazy. On Sundays, she spread out a tablecloth
on the grass with food for herself
and Higdon before they were married.
She read Russian novels by a kerosene lamp
at night and worked in a hosiery mill all day.
The steppes rolled out west to Jackson
and Memphis and Arkansas.

She was my mother's aunt.
She and her five sisters would send us
children socks and five dollar bills for Christmas.
One year, she gifted my brother and me
with packages of Davy Crockett underwear
which added to my coonskin cap
and my sister's Davy Crockett pup tent
that we pitched in the back yard.

I recall her mostly from my teens
when she lived across the street
from her sister Tillie and their ninety-six-year-old
mother. Higdon was long dead; she had no children.
She widow waltzed over the asphalt,
nearly getting hit by passing cars many times.
A child's smile on her face,
her conversations spiraled into non sequiturs
until she lost contact with everyone.

Mr. Turner

A long passenger train of laughter "ha, ha, ha-ed"
down the tracks through green woods east of London.
He was headed to the ferry for Margate. There the
twilights rhapsodized in ocher as the fishermen tied up
their boats after a day of casting and gathering nets.
His face was burned by the salt wind into the red that
visited it in a storm a few nights before when
vaudevillians smashed cherry tarts into a faux painting
of his in a theatrical revue. Here he had a room
overlooking the North Sea and domesticity
with Mrs. Booth.

In London galleries, he overheard snobbish
intelligentsia and bourgeois gawkers mock his art.
Upon viewing the fireworks of his sunset above vessels
of the Royal Navy, Queen Victoria cried, "Turner has
no respect for form. " But he ignored them all. He
imagined his critics choking on their contempt at white
linen tables in Knightsbridge as he spit onto his canvass
and continued painting. He found art in the pulse of
underclass Chelsea streets.

Beneath Woolen Heavens

After taking the wrong right turn, we drive down
this August day's baking asphalt in Dundalk, Md.
It was here fifteen years ago that Whitaker Chambers
had his biblical revelation telling him to leave
the Communist church for the Calvinist one of the
Republican party - swollen with files of gray flannel
sociopathy. We are going home from Memorial stadium
where Mayor D'Alessandro addressed the crowd before
the Orioles lost to the Yankees, again.

Finally, my father finds the correct route through this
1950's circle of the Inferno and we're headed southeast
into downtown to pick up my mother and sister in front
of Hutzler's where they had spent the afternoon
shopping for back to school clothes. They hop in from a
sidewalk resounding with the native accents of
Balamerese* which imprinted my brain and captured
my vocal cords from the age of four. Then we're riding
along the sea-green waters of the simmering Patapsco –
a river no one would ever mistake for the Seine. We
tour the barren province of Edgemere and its
bedraggled neighborhoods prior to arriving at
Sparrow's Point where my dad works
at the Dupont plant.

*Balamerese – the English language as pronounced
by Baltimore's citizens.

On Ritchie Highway going south, we turn off at Brooklyn Park. We stop there to look for winter suits at Robert Hall's ("this season will show you the reason – low overhead, low overhead"). At last we've made it back home to Harundale and Howdy Doody beaming from our RCA along with Princess Winter, Fall, Summer, Spring; Buffalo Bob, Flub-A-Dub and Mr. Bluster who our elderly neighbor – a floor walker for a department store – unwittingly impersonates from time to time.

Meanwhile, Chambers – years into his piety – walks around the acreage of his farm, thirty-eight miles north in Westminster, Md. He is retired now from his job as an editor at TIME. In the Piedmont swelter, he ambles over to the place in the field where he buried the Pumpkin Papers. Pacing back and forth, he thinks back to his disdainful father, his suffocating mother, and his tall, dark brother who was popular and towered over him like Hiss. The House on Un-American Activities is a static memory of grating, microphone testimonies now. Alger Hiss is trying to clear his name and Richard Nixon is Vice-President. He telephones William F. Buckley and talks for hours.

One evening, he plants religious-conservative visions in his diary until he begins to nod off. He goes to bed looking forward to an early frost in September to break the muggy heat. He dreams of right wing pundits rising from the soil across America like a grade B horror movie showing at a drive-in. He foresees a 24 hour cable TV news channel whose reportage tilts to the right until it is a phantasmagoria. He dozes on, a Halloween smile creeping onto his face.

My Grandparents Relive the Last Century

I've driven one wheel of my subcompact over the curb, trying to park in the overcrowded, caffeinated bohemia of twenty-first century Capitol Hill. "Ach, ach, use your head," my German grandfather exclaims through the reverb of my neural circuits. "But don't be stupid and park too far away from the curb or your midget car will get side swiped by one of those armored personnel carriers also known as AWD Sports Utility Vehicles that take up half a side street."

By an open, second-story window, my grandmother sits in her easy chair - her face half in shadow. Below, engines rev as the traffic threads by buildings sepia in the Queens twilight. She listens to the dark - ringing with the voices of her teenage sons getting off the Fresh Pond Road El station in 1935. But it is forty years later and they live in Delaware and Ohio. Her husband is many years dead. Her gin–rummy-playing lady friends have retired to Florida. She hears their laughter in the breeze from Sheep's Head Bay.

A pale, green plastic duck - that one of the neighbor children left there this morning - glows in the corner of the living room. She had somehow passed it by when her vacuum cleaner harmonized this morning's Lutheran hymns in German. I hear her, over the years, muttering "ach, ach," as she puts it on the coffee table, so as to not spoil her hausfrau ideal of uncluttered living space. Its luminous color reminds her of April and the linden trees of her New Jersey girlhood.

Souvenir Sidearm at the Luncheon on the Grass

The sideways profile of her pale orchid flesh glows
as she turns to look toward the artist. At this picnic
under the shadowy gestures of maples, she feels
estranged by the two black waist-coated students of art
discussing tone and perspective. Their conversations
remind her of the dry, chalk filtered light of classrooms
and the Parisian indifference of the Academy's main
floor crowded with student painters and their easels.

The student with the tasseled cap has placed a
souvenir pistol by his side to wave at curious strangers
and random Philistines who might enter this secluded
clearing. He has taken this empty-chambered gun –
which he has never fired – from the mantelpiece this
morning. It's a memento he bought from an eye-
patched stranger in the simmering gumbo air of New
Orleans last summer. He brought it back to impress his
friends along with raconteur tales of bourbon nocturnes
in Crescent City drinking establishments and for
fending off pickpockets in the streets. Its silver barrel
matches the flask of brandy next to the basket of
peaches that lies upon the woman's cast-off dress.

The men spend the lunch hour discoursing on the
limits of Naturalism, wondering if it should be
overthrown and what would then replace it.
Meanwhile, a woman in an off-white undergown is
rising to wash her ankles in the glassy stream behind
them. Its waters reflect the variegated hues of the open
field beyond. Speaking of line and contour and

color values, the self-important fop drones on to his vassal audience of one. He pays no attention to the green languor of the summer leaves that shade them. The feminine forms among them breathe out like exotic blooms on an alternate wave length.

The Wrong One

She came to the program - late autumn 1975 -
a white woman with an Afro – dark chestnut -
and an apple blossom face that bore
a faded X carved into the left cheek.
She lived a few miles from the center
edging black Avondale
under the smudged himmel of Cincinnati
that drifted automobile exhaust
and smoke from the breweries.

She was an artist and drew hooded figures in white,
darkening their faces with a magic marker. One day,
she showed me a sketch of hers from art class –
a charcoal interior breathing
like a time-lapsed photograph.
Later, she told me and a friend
about the year she spent in a commune
in British Columbia amid the druid vapor of hemlock
forests and how she did acid so many times she lost
count. Now, she was studying to be a Mormon
like her convert sister and one night
I went with her to one of their meetings
but couldn't relate to their marble certainties.

After I left the program, I called her
for a while but she played closed mouth.
Finally, I went to visit her in the hospital
where in the fluorescent pallor
with piercing sienna eyes,
she asked me to leave.
We were both 28 and liked poetry and the same music
but she didn't like me that way.

So I drove home that humid evening
with a heartsick condition
under the amber grimacing
of a warm second-rate-beer sun.
Sometime that night, I dreamed
of the travel-brochure blue skies
of Seattle and peaks that gleamed
with snow ringing white-winged cries.

Ballad of a Demon Cat

Just then the rooms turned to night;
thunder like a giant fist
hammered at the basement door
as our house cat hissed.
"I'll teach you to lock me down here,"
she said, "while the heaven
of a salmon casserole is
wafting from the oven."
We heard her heaving calico
body and her fierce call,
while her eyes swirled green as
Galway sky in a squall.
Running can openers and
drawing from ATMs
she said was the only reason
she could see for humans.

She said, "I can be quite pleasant-
a furry and sublime,
tiny, Xanaxed ex-tyrant
if I get what I want."

"Pay attention now, or, each
sundown, All Hollows' Eve
will fall upon your feeble world
without chance of reprieve."
"Out of my chair," she harangued
when someone was in it
on those binge watching worthy days
of Animal Planet.
She had the voice of the four winds
dark and brimming with hail
whirling from Kinsale to Derry

in a high banshee wail.
"You'll listen to me," she bawled
"because I have control
of your ho hum minds, now fetch me
that salmon casserole."

Ticket to the Deep

Admit four swimmers, it said.
The father and his three blond children
headed for the beach on an inlet
south of Baltimore's shipyards.
"We're going to the deep water,"
the towering patriarch joked
and Jamie Cipher, the middle child,
heard the reverb of his Brooklyn-accented jest
across the blue-green distance
as his tall figure swam to the horizon.

"Whose dinghy is that," one of Jamie's
two friends exclaimed – surveying its paint peeled
husk along a cove of the Severn river.
"Want to go to the other shore?" they asked,
grabbing stray boards to use as paddles.
Jamie sat in the middle, freezing with
the February cold and fear of drowning.
On the other side, he found a swan's egg
which he cracked seven years later.
It contained his slightly older self:
Panik the painter-eyed.

"Here's the merchandise," a friend said,
placing a green tablet in cellophane on his desk.
"Be careful, it's cut with speed," he advised.
The next day, Jamie took the admit to an inner ocean.
Beneath the surface, the sea creatures
became radiant Tibetans – dead for a thousand years.
The winter sun through his window receded,
an ancient eye over the colorless
cemetery lawns of suburban Cincinnati.

He flipped through magazine pages of breathing
women and listened to blues-rock structures
disintegrate and coalesce over and over until
he reached for the flotsam of Chlorpromazine.

Years later, James Cipher lived amid plaster walls
like empty canvasses, with a stream of jangled
Expressionist portraits flowing through his mind.
He paced back and forth, rattled by laughter
of misanthropic circus clowns
parading down the sidewalks.

Postcard Monologue – Lisbon

Castelo De Jorges

With others, I climb the sunny lane
past stucco walls of tendril draped balconies
and shops selling key chains and Kodak film.
At 38 degrees latitude, the Iberian azure
colors the pavement a granular teal.
It's Tuesday and around the corner wait
the hawkers of Fiera de Ladra in their tattered finery;
a litter of real and dubious curios at their feet,
they stand beckoning from either side –
wearing ersatz gold bands like those that once
reflected in Ferdinand Pessoa's eyes.

Dead Kings and Princes

I'm in the Old Palace of the Patriarch of Lisbon,
headed to the Pantheon – drawing room of the dead
royalty where the assassinated King Carlos with two
bullets in his heart lies in ashes in a crystal-topped urn.
His brother Prince Alfonso rests in the velvet interior
of a silver coffin weighed with 600 kilos of doom.
All these centuries of sovereignty crowd
this long chamber of sumptuous oblivion.

Bodegon Grill

Around 5 p.m., I come, hungry, to the Hotel Fenix
from the singing wires of the trolley line.
In the dining room, I look over at a corner table;
some natives say that there are late evenings
when you can see transparencies of Pessoa
flicker above the starched white cloth.
He sits there at odd moments with a glass
of Port and regales his heteronyms.

Jardiem Estrela

At the end of a palm lined walk, I see
the great domed church whose bells ring
out to strangers and aesthetes to survey
Portuguese art restored by Manuel Da Costa.
Later from the terrace, I get a nice view
of the Tagus clouded by ocean breezes;
I watch its deep mauve flow to the Atlantic
where night enfolds horizons that Pessoa once
dreamed.

Josef Kaputski

"Ach, Ach, those mahogany wing tips of mine," he
hisses. "I always wear black shoes, but the store was
out of that color when I shopped there last."
Josef hurries around a clock face inlaid in cement
along a 1939 Manhattan street
in a swarm of trouser-cuffed businessmen and
high heeled stenographers who are all taller than him.
He rushes beside them, his strident
blue eyes five feet above the sidewalk.
All are headed to the subway entrance
under a four-thirty sky.

While they hurtle through a tunnel to Brooklyn,
tears of childhood memories well in his eyes
for moments but fade
in the fluorescent din of passage.
"I could have studied the Classics
or Descartes and Schopenhauer," he mutters to himself.
"Yet, I wound up in the Department of Education.
Then for a few years, I taught grade school Latin and
Math amid paper airplane sorties and fist fighting
nine-year-olds. So I left to drive an electric bread truck
that went four miles an hour down
Bushwick's avenues."

In his twenties, he had nearly drowned
in the delirium of a typhoid fever.
Later, he married and became a pint-sized drudge
wisecracking to himself and his wife.
Now in his mind, he sees the flat green
East River he's been watching for
twelve years as an operator of the city's bridges.

Descending the stairs of an El station in Queens,
he worries the three blocks home about the light bill
and a case of empty club soda bottles in the kitchen.
He climbs the steps of his second story apartment
to a hausfrau heaven of pot roast and potatoes.
After dinner, he leafs through the Herald Tribune –
retreating to the funnies to chuckle at
Poor Arnold's Almanac burlesquing American history.

Sailing to Charlotte and the Next Sea

Wrought iron patterns of 4 p.m. shadow
and light on wooden walks of the pier recede,
as he looks west into the teal green expanse.
Empty cradle cries of gulls usher
him from a Liverpool dissonance
skirling with drunken bagpipers,
as the cities' church bells toll passengers
out to sea on the wind driven ship.

Diamond clear light until black spirals of storm
appear in crescendos over
the amniotic, swelling Atlantic
before he's reborn on the Carolina coast
with his father's name of Berryhill.
He travels inland over the Piedmont to Charlotte
where he scans the Appalachians
towering on the horizon
like slate blue waves standing still.
His descendants cross the mountains
over dirt roads winding through pine forests
of chord changes on frailing banjos,
into the undulant hills of Tennessee.

I awake from the dying generations
two centuries later in a town
south west of St. Louis and am taken
east to Delaware and Maryland.
Then I'm driven toward the setting sun
along the electric river dirge of the Ohio
to the rock 'n' roll conflagration of a Midwest city
with a dark angst in 4/4 time sounding in my blood.

My mind burns in a solitary retreat for years
until I hop a 747 and fly
northwest to a foggy metropolis
and hitchhike to a Pacific shore
where white birds call out
from salty waves accessing a child's
aether in my brain.
Then I'm lulled by surf rolling in
from an Orient
where it is always a new dawn.

The Nightingale, the Traitor

put desire in the youth's head
for an immortal woman
who was like a Tarot he misread
that spun him in self-deception.

The "vineyards" she left behind
bore gray grapes hard as pebbles
and the trees held no place for the wren
on its boughs weighed with apples
that overnight turned to stone.

She left him "half a city"
of Pre-Raphaelite strangers
who could not comprehend what he said
and other dark streets that proffered
a procession of Hamlet's dead.

"The Nightingale, the traitor"
wanted the youth's wounded eyes
to pour with the moonlight on the hill
where he reposed with blighted sighs
drowning in the bird's cold trills.

And he would sleep there for years,
his heart deep in widowerhood
through the fires and veils of all days
and hear the woman in a white mood
humming a night song far away.

A Coin in the Autumn Sky

In the maples this morning,
twilight colors hang on
as remnants of the season.
In the air's solar warmth,
they splatter on the lawn
at 1023 Columbia
that fronts the aquamarine
two story faux-Victorian.

Yellow nimbus of an oak
grows thin across the street
amid smartphone talk and tweets.
A silver Hyundai
pulses with hip-hop beats
as a willow bows its gold tresses,
tarnished and indiscreet,
to a gaggle of passing feet.

In the museum, a church
rises in sobriety –
white among a copse of trees.
Their shade casts September
across the land and leads
to a forest of birches wrapped round
in green Boa finery
like the faithful of Germany.

At La Push, the Pacific
rushes toward the crowd in
blue waves of adrenaline.
The sea stacks fade to black
along the horizon

where an ocher half coin winks farewell
before the next ascension
of October constellations.

Evidence of the Namesake Poet

No letters arrive for the poet
in his House and nothing sent from him
since 1982, though his face looks out
everywhere here - encased in glass.
At nine in Sunday clothes, he smiles
from a family photo in 1933.

In his books on the shelves,
you hear his everyman's voice
recite the blue highway scenes of Montana
diverging from the blare and roar
of I-90's semis and big rigs.
He speaks of Philipsburg
and the other towns
where the "could've beens"
start drinking at noon.
Then he's back on the asphalt
in a Plymouth Volare
he bought with poetry prize money –
his mind pitched to a bourbon note.

In a Motel 6 sleep, he travels
to the Angus coast of Scotland
in the mid-nineteenth century.
His waist-coated grand uncle,
an alienist, holds a top hat –
his pewter-gray hair ragged
with wind off a silver bay to the east.
Behind him, his charges roam and jabber
on the lawn of a Victorian asylum
while lines in his forehead appear
with the trouble like rain
confided in him every day.

Now he's in this First Hill school,
having left his wife in Missoula
and absented the Mission Range
darkening The Kicking Horse Reservoir
that held a dead lady in its depths.
Down a vacant corridor here,
his voice comes through
in an invisible cloud
of Hail Marys chanted by the ghosts
of ex-alcoholic priests.

Asleep in Weimar (After two drawings by Max Ernst)

She had a seizure
and lay back in a chair,
in a peach-colored dress,
in a sleep of white poppies.
Her Tajik manservant hovered near;
at her feet, a miniature green
dragon with a tongue of fire
licked the parlor air which grew
tremulous in her nodding dream.

Her sober-suited fiancé
looked through the white-veiled
window at the busy street
from where he and the servant
had carried her
after the sunlight flashing
in women's mirrors there began to hiss
and whirl in her private cataclysm.

Now, she has lost her money and servant
and her fiancé to typhoid.
She reclines - her mother-of-pearl body
exposed on a hillside
across the river from Weimar.
On the other side, a mob
is tramping down the cobblestone
overlooked by the ramparts of cathedrals.

She recalls a day last week
when she blacked out
and later woke to a coiling throng
of leather feet and Teutonic eyes
focused on her trouble.

They pronounced it "the work of the devil"
with the zeal of their Lutheran righteousness;
she made it home
through a gauntlet of epithets –
feeling naked in the crowd's derision.

Suddenly, the mob has reached the bridge
which begins to collapse
as she comes to in the parlor.

Last Odysseys (After Keats)

How impossibly beautiful the light
fell on the sea-green Channel
Keats crossed that day with Joseph Severn.
The high sun, a winking spy,
measured the decline of his breath.

Rattling across the plains of Germany,
he choked on dust
swirling into the coach
but kept his eyes open to visions.
On a hill, he saw a twelve-
year-old girl tied to a cross
with milky roses at her silk slippers.
A white Lutheran church
stood out like a sentinel
in a field fringed by blue
cornices of distant mountains.
Within a corridor of birches,
an agate stream flowed
into a like-colored river.

Flitting through the clouds
above Vienna, a woman appeared –
lying back in a boudoir chair
with a night-dark snake on her shoulder
and translucent breasts falling from
her ebony, opened robe.
In a garrison room,
the condemned man – flanked
by an army guard – waited
with a torn bible and the remains
of a last meal at his feet.

John W. Gorski

All the while, a clock face
obscured in the Austrian overcast
burned to remind the poet.

As Severn attended him,
the yellow sun of Rome
fevered through the window
and began to fade like cries
along the Tiber where boats
and buildings floated away.

The Schadenfreude Sisters

They lived in the castled heights
of a swank suburb
on a hill above Milwaukee.
They were sophomores
when I was a freshman
at our public high school.
I was short in my oxford button-
down shirts and khakis
and they were inches taller
in white blouses and plaid skirts.
They looked down on me
under blonde and tawny bangs –
their unblemished faces
featuring Germanic scowls.

"Yah, yah and nah, nah,"
they would sing as they passed me in the hall.
"Mel, the mental midget,
needs a girlfriend
but who would want him," they chorused.

They went to choir practice
after classes and would emerge
giggling in cream cheese voices
about the cute boys
they hoped would ask them out.
Chattering homeward down the sidewalks,
they suddenly broke into
a song by the Shangri-las
but their Brill Building aspirations
would never make it past
our high school talent show.

In a few years, they went off to college
where their mirthful schadenfreude faded
with the British Invasion
as everyone's hair got longer
and wardrobes turned paisley.

To and Fro in Fugue Time

She became a still pebble
at the cool, river bottom of sleep
and then wrapped in a bed sheet –
her midnight-indigo hair
draping her bare shoulders,
she peered through the windows
of her low income building.
She saw the looking glass stream
recording cumulus, as it flowed by
the distant, blue shrub mountains of Santa Fe.
Her vision had grown to a wider terrain
after she discontinued the Ativan.

Now she wakes in a white gown
in the flames of her twilight bedroom
glimpsing an ashtray of stubbed-out Larks.
Something's out of place
and her brain simmers
with the half bottle of wine
she drank a few hours ago.

She hears knock, knock and clawing sounds. "It's Mrs.
Cherry from down the hall. Rise and shine, it's 7 PM."
"Oh right," she thinks to herself,
"Mrs. Cherry, the etiquette freak
with Dirty Denko, her pet armadillo
who the old woman is teaching to brush his teeth.
She's lonely and probably just wants to talk
about the liquor store hold up a block over."

But suddenly, she falls
into another drowsy journey
and dreams of 5 a. m. linden-
green air-conditioned light
chilling a window where a stone owl
looks in with one eye pried
open by a shadowy jeweler.
Then she rouses to an aging
Zoloft voice singing, "Come along,
come along" to the far away
whimper of the armadillo.

Visiting the Fatherlands

The sky was losing azure
above ragged miles
of dissenting, cumulus broadsides -
printed in Slovakian –
that seemed to cry out:
"You don't belong with us."
Chilled ocher infused
those low, February clouds
and the meadow air I walked through
toward two skeletal poplars
and a rich man's house in the distance.

Between the trees,
bits of light pealed
giggles across a stream
that a storybook quarter moon
looked back upon
with a cynical smile.

I approached
the three-story manor house
and its front windows
lucent with pie-faced,
ginger-haired children
who laughed and sneered.
Their muted, Bratislava voices
seemed to mouth the phrase,
"You're trespassing here."

So I passed them by,
returning on an unmarked road

to the Danube plains
under dumb struck heavens
until I reached a village
with a wayfarer's hotel.
There I read the story
of the Prodigal Son
between black cardboard covers
under the lunar parody
of a single glowing bulb.
At last, the kilowatts
faded into the vermillion
revelation of morning
and I was freed from the lonely
embrace of a dream.

Obituary Buzz

Seven hundred miles away,
he had a stroke and six months
later, my grandmother finally
told us he was winding
down a Poe maelstrom
where people he'd known since childhood
no longer had their given names.
The streets and houses
of his hometown seemed
from a gothic novel
he had neglected to read.
So he would sing along
to the local Top 40 radio station
playing "Meet The Beatles."

The next morning,
we got another call
and that afternoon, my mother
boarded a plane for a funeral
in Middle Tennessee.
After school that day,
I walked along the path
by the railroad tracks
running south from Baltimore
and told the bees
of Severna Park, Maryland.
I trusted them to buzz the news –
to an invisible firmament –
that an Adams patriarch
had flown past the billion-
winged din of a lifetime.

Months later when I visited
Murfreesboro in the warm
drawl of July breezes,
Grandmother would relate
how Grandfather appeared
in fleeting moments
that seeped into the hall
like a cold November morning.

Was It a Party?

No one was waving to us
from those Miller Time-lit windows
as a school friend and I drunkenly stared
from balmy, October shadows
that evening in nineteen sixty-two.
His older sister and pals there
rocked to the Beach Boys with mid-shipmen
from the Naval Academy
and madras attired teens
whose eyes flashed superiority.
I was five-six standing straight
up in my penny loafers,
so they bore me aloft on a whim
out to the front yard while my brain swam.
That was the night I met my double -
the socially ill-fitting Vern -
in that WASP abode in Pines on the Severn.

Was it a party
or a prank excuse?

So Dave asked me over
to his unit in Holly Park
early one night in nineteen seventy-nine
and like any monotone lark,
I accepted the invitation.
It was a dead mid-winter evening
closed by a gray Durer ceiling
that had lingered months too long
till we arrived and his wife
offered a couple hits on a bong.
Our food stamp, stoner friends there
grooved to "Bodhisattva"

from the Dan's "Countdown to Ecstasy"
while time lolled indifferently.
As we returned north on I-5,
starlight poured from speeding cars
and Dave's tape deck played "Spiders From Mars."

Was it a party
or substance abuse?

Part III

Unfinished Collage 1972

European Vagabond

Bare trees on the January horizon,
a few Dutch houses and barns
scattered over this lowland
where Johanna walks
a sere finger of land edged
in dead grass and frozen canals
lit blue by the weak specter above.
She sees the old woman trudging ahead
in a cold, Protestant distance
with a bible in her right hand
and wonders: what is the purpose?
And then she decides to leave
Holland where she was born.

Traveling over the plains of Saxony,
she passes a faux crucifixion
along the road to Leipzig.
An adolescent girl
in a long, gray satin dress
is tied to the cross as a grown man
kneels in adoration by her sandaled feet
but Johanna has no resonance anymore
with this symbol of her childhood belief
and proceeds as an aqua hue
seeps into the middle of the heavens.

In the opium dark
of an artist's studio in Berlin,

she poses in a chair –
her luminous breasts
hanging between her opened robe.
An ebony snake winds around
her torso and to her left shoulder
where it looks out and hisses
in Morse code at the artist.
During this shadowy session,
Johanna suddenly hears
a seagull cry out from Marseilles.

Time is Liquid

Watching the pleasure boats
drift on the acrylic gray
waters of Lake Union,
I talk for hours this day
with my friends, Don and Maury –
two long-time musicians.
We inhale July clouds
and exhale memories
of forty years past
in Cincinnati.

We remember the fire
breathing hallways of the brain
and the sunlight speaking
Sanskrit in the refrain
of traffic on Calhoun Street
in waves through summer heat.
The Rossetti figures
of girls my friends knew
appear once again
in a fading hue.

Time is liquid
on this slow afternoon,
looking back on years
like a procession
of forgotten runes.

We laugh at each other
and call ourselves old men
just trying to regain
our youthful oxygen
from an overheard chord change
somehow new and strange.
And sometimes we still hear
ventilation systems
fill with the choiring
of guitar anthems.

Dizzy

On a quiet afternoon walk,
you forget who you are
under a monotone winter sky
that takes whispers and conversations
into its gray cumulus.

The thought balloon
above your head is empty –
a sphere floating away
from you and the outstretched
bony arms of oaks and maples.

From a nearby telephone line,
a winter smart aleck
in coal-black feathers cries out
"Your mind is going bye-bye."
"Mind your own business,"
you shout back like
a Russell Edson character
through the caw, caw, caw serenade.

Unfinished Collage – 1972

A winter tree grows
above the grease paint
gleaming on the face of the clown –
a cast off saint.
He looks into the unseen
mirror for the taint
that ostracizes him
to the edge of the crowd's
hissing continuum.

A young man runs by
the tree toward dawn –
his graphite-black breathing shadow
soon to be gone.
When he wakes, he will
be merely a pawn
fighting the traffic
of doubt filling his head
with its warring panic.

Why did that stricken-eyed
clown rise over and over
in my mind's eye
all those mornings of my twenties
under a solitary sky?

On the other side
of the tree, a shroud
adorns a war protester

wailing aloud.
Marmoreal in his robes
daubed in blood red,
he watches a caption
left writhing on this scene
of no resolution.

Pet Sounds Revisited

Through the mask of age,
a 60-year-old Brian Wilson
looks back at the blue
Pacific of his youth
while playing a concert in London.
His eyes gleam with the sun
lighting the long rolling waves
on Redondo Beach
where he hung out in his teens.

In the cedar forests
east of Lake Washington,
we watch the genius
recreate his master synthesis
backed by the Wondermints
on cable TV.
Having entered the room
from a cumulus of smoke,
I ascend like the evergreen
trees into the halcyon
of a Northwest sky.
My musician friends dissect
the performance and compare
it to the original disc
noting the cornucopia
of instrumental flourishes.

We relive the Venusian blondes
and blue-green roar
of the surf Brian sings about,
as the music rises
to the theremin heavens.

How Hot Was It? (July 1970)

The sun set brick red
above the ovens
of downtown Cincinnati
that the river simmered
past on its way downstream
in the subtropical heart
of the Ohio River valley.

Eight miles north in College Hill,
it was no better that furnace evening
two weeks before we had
air conditioning installed.

We watched a telecast
of the Reds playing the Pirates
in Pittsburgh – another
urban sauna to the east.
And then the 11 o'clock news
flashed its home break ins,
murders and baseball scores
from our RCA,
as the dark sky hung
like a blanket
just removed from a washing machine.

Later in the middle
of Johnny Carson's monologue,
Ed McMahon called out:
"How Hot Was It?"
"It was so hot," Johnny said
"that the Westwood Fire Department
was called out to hose down
the UCLA football practice squad."

Back home in Cincinnati,
it was so hot that
our domestic short hair cat,
looking for a cool place to sleep,
meowed at the refrigerator door.

Rimbaud in London

In an amber-lit tavern in Soho,
the alphabet revealed
its rainbows to him
between heavy clouds of absinthe –

the black of his mother's pronouncements
and flies buzzing around a dead man
along a road in Ardennes,

the white of clerics' collars
around their bulging necks
in the hours of their hypocrisy,

the infernal red of his arguments
with Verlaine lighting windows
down a foggy street,

the cerulean lamplight above Charleville
that shone in his earliest days,

the green waves of the Mediterranean
that called to him
over the metal and tin rattle
of the street's consonants
and the cold murmur of the Thames.

Red Grooms' Pictures

Manhattan

Buses and cabs like plastic toys
spill forward from the asphalt
of the Lower East side's dawn streets
under rainbows of eatery signs
and walk ups reaching to
the borough's smoky ceilings.

Commuters roar through
the Dostoyevsky underground
reading the Daily News
in the electric lights of the gray-green cars.

On an evening train,
Flower Power figures and Harlem dandies
ride to 14th street where they whirl
on a subterranean carousel.

The Unicorn Strikes Back

The moon pale unicorn spears
the brown dog sent to bite him,
with another one snarling on his shoulders.
He kicks back at the enemy soldiers
with swords and crossbows aimed
at those who would proceed
from the walled city.

In the background, the green sea
bobs with foreign ships
delivering their forces.

A silent crow, perched in a pear tree,
watches foppish nobles blowing hunting horns
as an old beggar points a yellowed finger
at the mythical creature.

At the gate to the city,
a white queen waits
before a silver crowd of knights.

John Donne – Pyrford and Beyond

In Pyrford, the poet's house
stood by the Wey River –
stopped as a stillbirth.
It's green waters mirrored a weak sun
winking like an invalid in bed
and the winter trees along it
gaunt as the limbs of his children.

He had come out of Fleet Prison
for marrying Anne
against her father's wishes.

For years they lived in that house,
where his wife bore twelve children
and they had to accept charity;
he wrote poems for his patrons
amid scampering bare feet
and a gaggle of mouths to be fed.
As an older man they came back
to him – aspen-faced
and twitching in multiple fevers.

On a December afternoon,
the four o'clock sun
had spent its last rays;
then when the night had taken the hour
into its measureless black vault,
he wrote a poem upon
the death of his daughter Lucy.
He spoke of the young lovers to come

and remembered when he was
one of them – his head filled
with the dark sky, his thoughts
lost in an horizon of the grave.

Metro Interlude

A camera eye pans the strip
mall highway the 12:15
is passing by under a Pacific shroud
left over from the morning.

Inside, I listen to voices
in waves rolling in and out.
"What am I doing right?"
"I don't know."
"What am I doing wrong?"
"I don't know."
"I lived in Honduras for a year,
It's always warm and green there
though the ground is a carpet of spiders."
"I seen him in his casket
but it wasn't him,
he partied with everyone in that band;
I don't see how it happened."

"Eha"s– the six pack of Corona laughter
from two day laborers resounds
from seats in the back.
"Sometimes, I feel like
I'm a hundred years old,"
a thirty-year-old man says.
"Deep thoughts," his companion replies.
"But I can still get the young chicks,"
he reassures those around him.

The static sky grows dolorous
with synthesizer music
from someone's smartphone
and we are headed out to sea.

Little in Common – A Brief Count of Skirmishes

There was something endearing
in her umber, wallflower eyes
when I first caught them looking at me in an aisle
of artificial light in a UW office
as we placed six-digit requisitions in file folders.
We talked for months about music we liked
and what we did on the weekends
until I finally asked her out.

Then I was over at her condominium in Burien
every Saturday. Sometimes we went to movies
or the mountains or the Sound before
winding up at her place again with carryout food.
We listened to KZOK on the weekends
when they played the one hundred greatest
albums of all time - half of them by Led Zeppelin.
She liked AC/DC and Judas Priest,
although I saw them as Gothic hordes
from the eastern frontier and knew
that Ozzy Osbourne was no T. S. Eliot
or even an A. E. Housman.
At least, we both liked Pink Floyd and the Beatles
but everyone liked the Beatles except for Elvis
who, by that time, had already left the peanut
butter and banana sandwiches of Graceland with a
Dilaudid-compromised heart.
Then she would turn on MTV and we watched
Culture Club and Duran, Duran. She said

they were cute; I thought they were lightweights.
So we would drift away from the drone
of techno-pop to her bedroom.

"You always rank down the things I like,"
she used to say and then there was the time
my car broke down on the 1st Avenue S bridge
and I didn't call her prior to arriving two hours late
and got no response when I rang her door bell then
or when I called her from home that night.
We were tired of each other.

Months later, I missed the crazy heat of our flesh
together in the coconut fragrance of her room.
Months after that, I would wake
up in the charcoal void of 4 a.m.
and realize that I was a jerk.

Five Doorways to the Abyss

In the beginning, there was a roller coaster
screaming with faces I'd never seen,
a merry-go-round of them going by
on wooden ponies that pumped
to the guffawing of German Polkas.
Others rose on a Ferris Wheel
into the 8 p.m. Baltimore summer sky
to vanish for good in the carbon-breathing night.

The woman's eyes are averted,
her countenance hugging a concrete walkway
at a vacant train station in the foot hills
of an Austrian mountain range
where the disappearing rails hum into silence.

The young Parisian woman,
in a white dress is passed out
upon a mahogany floor
below shelves of burnt-sienna tomes
adding shadows to the library's
"rare books room" until all their knowledge
is obliterated by the dark.

A twenty-year-old girl has lain down
on the alfresco floor of a seaside wine bar
among empty silver chairs
and immaculate, glass table tops.
Her eyes are usurped by the blue,
crystal distance of the Mediterranean.

Selfie - 1977

It is my second summer in Seattle
and I'm reeling down to the deck
of a ferry crossing Puget Sound.
Agate-blue clouds smudge my face
in a vertigo whirling scenes of my past;
I see myself in darkening blond rays,
wearing 70's styles – twenty-nine forever.

Part IV

A City of Pre-Raphaelite Strangers

John W. Gorski

Artificial Light (After Hammershoi)

You come in now from these streets of misty night
after the November day's last encore
of invalid sun and the muted roar
of crowds wandering in Copenhagen gaslight.
Two candles wait at a table tonight
in a vacant alcove like a sepulcher
for patrons from a century before:
a man and wife rapt in quiet delight.
Amid the umber walls of this café,
you notice the interior's age
and where the two dined - lit in flint-gray -
conversing about the man's painted images
until one morning he passed away
leaving his enigma to walls and pages.

Prelude to a Bummer

By chance, a strange blond light
flashed through a stand of stunted trees
on this Scottish mountainside
suddenly warmed by a Marseilles breeze.
A woman on a horse
flew by with hair gold as a doubloon –
a ravishment of locks that somehow
cast the eerie spell of an autumn moon.
All that day, the young man
lay on his back in the high green meadow,
watching fleeting clouds figure
to Cupids with thoughtlessly drawn bows.
His brain was burning out
with the dying sun when the woman
came back, in the vanishing light,
wrapped in opalescence of a new moon.

She urged him up roads -
stone-studded - around the barren tors;
her silver voice promised
a far hill with an enchanted bower.
But he and the maid found
a cave of masked men and women
instead with acerbic tongues
that stabbed at the couple's bright vision.
And for minutes after,
they left those Schadenfreude shadows,
ridicule still followed
with its distant anthracite echoes.
As they walked westward
to the angry sea of Hebrides,
she said, "you must live in soot-
filled London quarters if you want me."

"And there for twenty years,
you will wait where the winter fogs burn
with coal smoke and rumor of sun -
your mind wanly fixed on my return."

"But you may catch my icy gleam, now and then,
as I spin laughing amid the constellations."

La Belle Dame Mary Jane (Apologies to Keats)*

Oh, what can ail thee, drab nebbish,
alone and wanly partying?
In the streets, patrons from Duck Island
like young loons sing.

Oh, what can ail thee, drab nebbish
of slowed down metabolism.
Christmas lights jewel the night streets
and adorn tree limbs.

I see the parchment of thy brow
scored with indelible lines.
In thy cheeks are hollow valleys
of age resigned.

I met a maid in Oceans Green
in the neon dark, a goth's child.
Her hair was cobalt, her face pale
and her eyes were mild.

She gave me a chocolate chip jazz
cookie for a ten dollar bill.
She said "that should get your weekend off
to a slow chill."

I hopped in my subcompact
and drove off with the un-zonked.
I saw Jazzercise and Vern Fonk
but forgot to honk.

At home in the wintry kitchen,
I munched the prescribed dose.
I waited for nearby shadows
to grow verbose.

I played a Leonard Cohen
CD in the dark living room.
I regarded his smoky trance
of romantic gloom.

He had returned to LA
from a snow-shouldered Zen mountain.
He was back in the hazy streets
and the arms of women.

I heard his account of Yahweh
chasing him around the Sinai.
Hebrew violins accompanied
his hunted cries.

Then suddenly, my thoughts were flying
eastward to a disorient.
There I heard the deeper chords in
the singer's lament.

So this is why I anguish here –
alone and wanly partying.
I need psychic calm for "I can't believe
I ate the whole thing."

*many apologies

Dumpster Diving with Jonathan Livingston Seagull

There is no use
in wheeling above this gentrified
Ballard pizza restaurant.
Many evenings, I scavenged here
with a motley of my brethren
when it was an Ivar's Seafood Bar.
I descended from a cirrus zone
years ago that shimmered
over steel and glass forests
of buildings reaching upward
with their babble of commerce.

Now I'm no stranger
to the Paradise Lost
of these downtown avenues
of tabloid scraps that pirouette
along the dirty sidewalks,
while people behind me harmonize:
"Why can't I be cool?
Why do I wake up
in a pillow full of drool,
worrying about paying my rent in Seattle?"

I know I've got to rise up
into the azure again
with the stirring Brooklyn tenor
of Neil Diamond's theme song
resounding in my ears.
Although I can't reach perfection,
I'll fly over the salty waves

and then make a right at Shilshole Bay
and later a left at Highway 99
to follow the other gulls
to the Bitter Lake Ivar's.
There the remains
of the Tuesday night special
of cod and chips await
my gourmet sensibilities.

Belgian Nocturne (After Magritte)

Three black-coated men
of the artist's
ontological society
stop in a Belgian meadow
to discuss anti-rationality.
They have strolled west
through these March fields
under the blue spell of this night
that quiets restless thoughts
in its cold pages of moonlight.

They had come from the east
where twenty years ago
a great charcoal bird,
talking Messerschmitt lingo,
flew over book burning fires
and perched in a loud shadow.

They are school masters
in an exile
from the clockwork lessons of their trade
in ink and paper classrooms
where dreaming minds are betrayed.
Three lunar crescents
are poised above
their bowler hats like bright emblems
of arcane philosophies
they speak of in starlit theorems.

The bird was flying back
into the smoky
gray Medieval skies
roiling the painter's vision,
leaving the villagers speechless
in a static of confusion.

Laundry Room Talk

So I'm ready to drop my blues
and grays into the machine and start
the percussion/bass cycle of wash/rinse/spin
when Maria wanders into
the basement fluorescence.
She asks what time the mail came yesterday
because she didn't receive any.

Then we're talking about parents
and how she grew up in the U District
in an Irish/Italian family
that was forthright with each other.
I tell her about the jumpy mathematician
who rode the El through Queens
and Brooklyn to his classes
and about the young woman
from Tennessee who spent evenings
journeying through book land
or painting galleries of irises.
I tell Maria of their meeting
in Missouri during World War II and how my
father's icy, city-wise vision jibed with the small-
town fires of my mother's idealism. I say they
should have never gotten married but she replies
that she's glad her parents did.

Next, we discuss creativity and depression
and how she thinks I use the dark factories
of my verse to block out blue skies.
She tells me she studied English

at the Jesuit school where she learned of
the black cloud hanging over Robert Frost.
Suddenly, I see her as a child lying in bed
while the aqua lamplight of a summer evening
pours into her window near Cowen Park;
her eyes are saddened by the knowledge
that her father will die when she is twenty.
Then, she is standing alone on a wintry Dublin
street – a child holding a silver camera in the night
as sea gulls rise through whirling snow
into the white above the river Liffey.

John W. Gorski

Stranger in a Strange Land of Ersters* and Clams

It was to that field I liked to escape
the juggernaut of banshee-crying students on noon
break the year our fifth-grade classes were held
in the Sunday school rooms
of Harundale Presbyterian church.

A four lane highway of seafood restaurants to the
west ran south from Balamer* alongside
the church and its bleached grass field,
to the north, that mimicked a recess yard.
Many clear days, I wandered over its stubble
to a pine grove bordered by the planned
community of pre-fab, Post-war housing
where I lived from grades one to six.
In the northeast corner, a shallow pond reposed -
fanning out from the dusty corner
of an invisible home plate.
There one cloud-mottled evening,
I first saw Mark who would become
my best friend in seventh grade.
He was throwing a ball as far as it
would reach into the Tidewater Maryland sky.
A ten-year old next to me said, "He's a maniac" –
a noun new and strange to me
in the latter half of those Eisenhower years
when broadcasts of the McCarthy hearings had
faded to be subsumed by television's
 barking Rin Tin-Tin and Lassie.

Yes, the pond where a group of older boys,
renegade monks in black leather,
threw me head first into the one-foot
deep murk of cold, March waters
because they assumed an instant superiority
to the "shrimp," blue-eyed albino of my person.
Then they went off to check in with the head monk
at his garage filled with hub caps they had stolen
for him.

In a nightmare sleep after that long day,
I saw myself materialize in old age –
wearing a striped, golf shirt on a Florida-green
lawn, almost as fat and bald as Rush Limbaugh.

*1 – The way oysters are pronounced in the
    Baltimore area.

*2 – How Baltimore is pronounced by its denizens.

Off Route

A yellow half-light sedates
the street she thought
she remembered in Capitol Hill
where she leans now against a bourbon-
colored building of dimming windows
rollicking twenty-year-old laughter.
Waiting for the interminable transit,
she feels agitated and then vague.

Under a linden-green beret
and long, dark-blond hair,
the creases and hollows
of her fifty-year-old face
fill in with the 11 p.m. dark.

When she doesn't go blank,
her mind goes back and forth
between this city and the rolling
farmlands of Eastern Washington.
She grew up there and recalls
a strange, phosphorescent
glow around everything.
She sees a gingko tree with leaves
buzzing like a golden storm of locusts.
She keeps hearing the severed
head of a baby doll wailing,
in the near-dawn hours,
abandoned next to a bicycle wheel
of bone-white tires

alongside a low, stone wall
topped by a few
empty "Ripple" wine bottles.

Her nerves tense like trip wires,
while she goes on waiting
for a way out of this alien interlude.
But the bus will never come
because the driver is dying
of cirrhosis of the liver
and the route was canceled last year.

Photo Album

From the psych ward rants
and nicotine ghosts
of Third Avenue,
I take the rainy transit
past horizons of cranes and condos
to the abandoned cinema
of drawn Venetians.
There I view
sixty-year-old Polaroids
of my mother and father
smiling beside the blue Delaware Bay.

Haiku Variant for Frank

Under Sinatra skies,
July breezes shine
with baubles of sunlight
shaded by his fedora.

John W. Gorski

Bio for John W. Gorski:

John was born in Missouri but lived most of his childhood and adolescence in Maryland and Ohio. He has lived in Seattle for the past forty years. He received a B.A. in English from the University of Cincinnati in 1974 and has taken poetry writing courses at the University of Washington Extension as well as the Hugo House in Seattle.

John's poems have appeared in Seattle area publications such as *Art Access, Paper Boat, The Metro Poetry Bus Project, Poems on Buses* (2014) and *Switched-On Gutenberg,* and most recently, in *Five Willows Literary Review.*

John's employment includes a number of clerical and custodial jobs over the years. He is currently retired.

www.ingramcontent.com/pod-product-compliance
Lightning Source LLC
Chambersburg PA
CBHW060124260626
47160CB00005B/2005